Animal ABC's

A Journey Through The Wild

A

is for Alligator
"A is for Alligator,
with a big toothy grin,
It swims through the water and
splashes right in!"

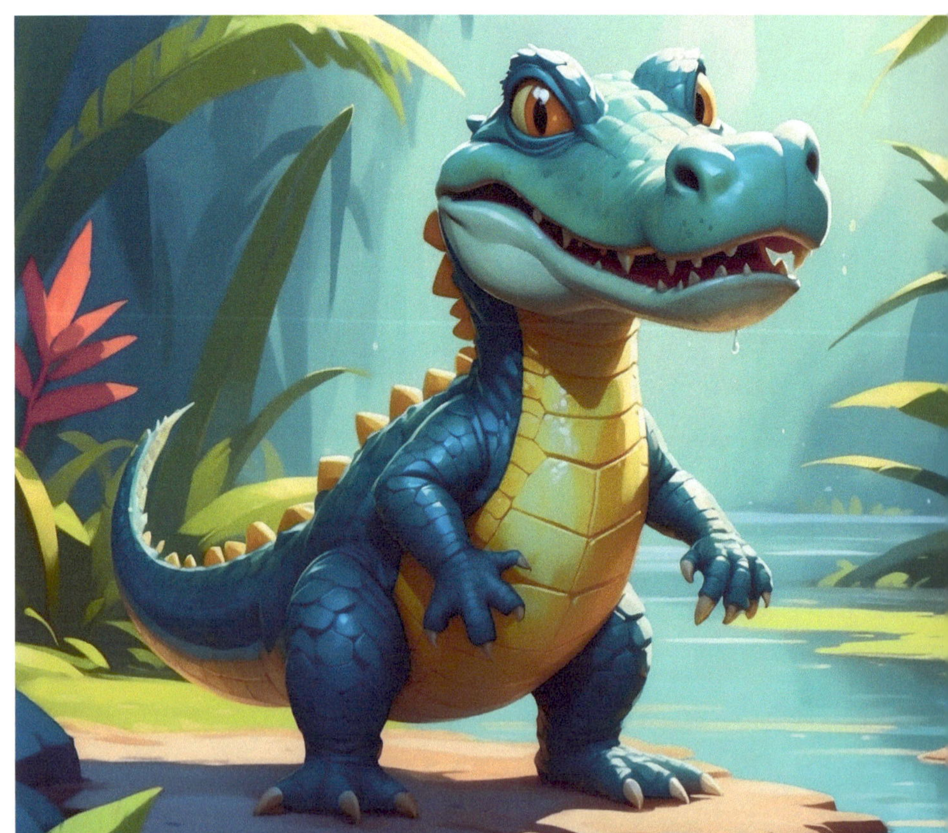

B

is for Bumblebee

"B is for Bumblebee,
buzzing by the flowers,
Collecting sweet nectar for
hours and hours!"

C

is for Cat
"C is for Cat,
so soft and so furry,
With a flick of its tail,
it dashes in a hurry!"

D

is for Dinosaur
"D is for Dinosaur,
from long, long ago,
Stomping through forests,
moving slow and low!"

E

is for Elephant
"E is for Elephant,
enormous and gray,
With big flappy ears and
a trunk that can spray!"

F

is for Frog

"F is for Frog,
leaping up high,
Catching flies with a hop
and a sly little eye!"

G

is for Goose
"G is for Goose,
with feathers so white,
Honking and waddling – what a
funny sight!"

 H

is for Horse
"H is for Horse,
galloping fast,
With a flowing mane
as it dashes past!"

I

is for Iguana
"I is for Iguana,
sunning on a tree,
Green and scaly,
as calm as can be!"

J

is for Jellyfish
"J is for Jellyfish,
drifting in the sea,
With long, wavy tentacles
flowing so free!"

K

is for Kangaroo
"K is for Kangaroo,
bouncing so high,
With a little joey
snug nearby!"

L

is for Lion
"L is for Lion,
with a powerful roar,
King of the jungle,
brave to the core!"

M

is for Monkey
"M is for Monkey,
swinging in the trees,
Chattering and laughing,
full of cheeky ease!"

N

is for Nightingale
"N is for Nightingale,
singing so sweet,
A melody at dusk,
a lovely treat!"

O

is for Owl
"O is for Owl,
wise and wide-eyed,
Hooting at night
as it watches the sky!"

P

is for Pig
"P is for Pig,
rolling in the mud,
With a curly tail
and a happy little thud!"

Q

is for Quail
"Q is for Quail,
with feathers so fine,
Scurrying through grasses
in a quick, zigzag line!"

R

is for Raccoon
"R is for Raccoon,
with a mask on its face,
Sneaking around with
a curious pace!"

S

is for Squirrel
"S is for Squirrel,
with a tail so fluffy,
Leaping through trees,
nimble and scruffy!"

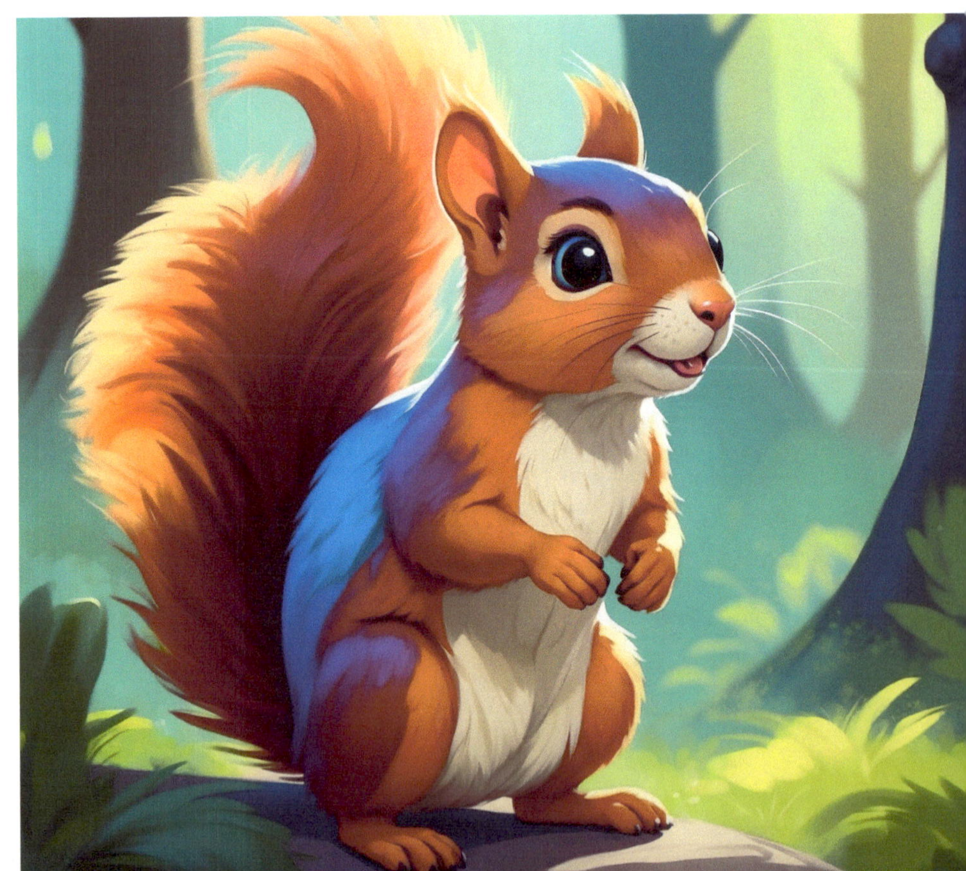

T

is for Turtle
"T is for Turtle,
slow and steady,
Carrying its home,
always ready!"

U

is for Urial
"U is for Urial,
with curved, strong horns,
Climbing steep mountains
as day breaks and dawns!"

V

is for Vulture
"V is for Vulture,
soaring up high,
With wings spread
wide across the sky!"

W

is for Whale

"W is for Whale,
giant and grand,
Spouting tall fountains,
the ruler of the sand!"

X

is for Xeme (Sabine's Gull)
"X is for Xeme, gliding with grace,
Wings spread wide in an open-air race!"

Y

is for Yak

"Y is for Yak,
sturdy and strong,
Woolly and warm,
trekking all day long!"

Z

is for Zebra
"Z is for Zebra,
with stripes of black and white,
Galloping in herds,
a wonderful sight!"